PAPER CASKETS

Emilia Danielewska

paper caskets

neWest press

NeWest Press wishes to acknowledge that the land on which we
operate is Treaty 6 territory and a traditional meeting ground and
home for many Indigenous Peoples, including Cree, Saulteaux,
Niisitapi (Blackfoot), Métis, and Nakota Sioux.

Library and Archives Canada Cataloguing in Publication

Danielewska, Emilia, 1990-, author
Paper caskets / Emilia Danielewska.
(Crow said poetry)
Poetry.
ISBN 978-1-988732-36-7 (softcover)
I. Title.
PS8607.A55647P37 2018   C811'.6   C2018-901754-6

Board Editor: Douglas Barbour
Cover design, digital collage & typesetting: Kate Hargreaves
Author photograph: Emilia Danielewska

NeWest Press acknowledges the Canada Council for the Arts, the
Alberta Foundation for the Arts, and the Edmonton Arts Council for
support of our publishing program. This project is funded in part by
the Government of Canada.

201, 8540 – 109 Street
Edmonton, AB T6G 1E6
780.432.9427
NeWest Press www.newestpress.com

No bison were harmed in the making of this book.
PRINTED AND BOUND IN CANADA

To honour NeWest Press' 40th anniversary, we've inaugurated a new poetry series to go alongside our Nunatak First Fiction, Prairie Play, and Writer as Critic series: Crow Said Poetry. Crow Said is named in honour of Robert Kroetsch's foundational 1977 novel *What The Crow Said*. The series aims to shed light on places and people outside of the literary mainstream. It is our intention that the poets featured in this series will continue Robert Kroetsch's literary tradition of innovation, interrogation, and generosity of spirit.

for Ciocia Zdzidzia

contents

part I

tintype children

laverna

Laverna, born and thrust into her mother's arms, umbilical noose still around her neck, her lips bruised blue. At the funeral the pallbearers, two uncles from her mother's side, balance the coffin on their fingertips. Petite Laverna buried inside the depths of a pink fleece blanket, only her face peeking through, a garland of wildflowers arranged around her body. The wind blows, the coffin rocks.

darkroom

Close the door behind you, don't let the light seep. Equipment cramped in each corner of the room, squeeze through to the sink, lay out four trays. Lick your fingers and tuck your hair behind your ears, let the water run lukewarm. Slip in feet first, dip and swish, she comes into view. Pluck her out, push her head back under. Again. Clothespin her with the others under the amber glow, grab another blank page. The water rises to the lip of the tub as his body sinks in. Swish, swish, wash his prints from the chemicals, scrub decay from his neck. A piece of twine from wall to wall, clip clip his glossy eyes, chalky cheeks. Drip dry.

alfred

He is already quite stiff when his parents bring him in. His mother had clothed him in a dress shirt and pants rolled at his ankles. Leather booties laced to his feet, the most difficult part of the whole ordeal, she confesses, but she wants him in his Sunday best. This will be his last photograph, after all. He passed yesterday, at two in the afternoon. Sick with pneumonia for the past few weeks. We grease back his hair, shiny, healthy. On the photograph I'll paint his eyelids white, add two blue pupils. We prop him up using a wooden stand I have in the studio, drape a little arm over a chair for extra support. Then we stage him with some flowers, like he's delivering them. The camera takes a few seconds to draw the portrait. Most kids I find difficult to keep still for so long. Not Alfred. They place him in a coffin directly after the shoot and pallbear him out the door.

gloria

Gloria was a house call. I brought my equipment in the evening and the parents set me up in Gloria's bed for the night. A spacious room on the second floor, high ceiling, a vague vinegar scent lingering from the floorboards. The wardrobe filled with folded cotton dresses. A shelf of porcelain faces with glass eyes hanging above my head. I slept well. In the morning two servants dressed in matching grey suits cart Gloria from the cellar to the drawing room, dress, undress, redress, her hair in rollers. Prop her in the stuffed lilac armchair, then the navy floral. I coordinate her limbs, reposition her arms, cross her ankles, loosen a piece of hair and let it fall across her shoulder, angelic. Scuttling servants bring tall vases from the foyer and rearrange them, from foreground to background. I situate myself behind the camera; wait for the sun to rise just above the windowsill, illuminate her linen skin and clothes.

violet

I'm not allowed near Violet. Her body, posed and propped on two praline cookie tins, greets me when I walk in through the door. Her parents dictate how far away my camera can be, at what angle I can stand, the set-up, her posture, the way her exposed hands drape across the front of her dress. She had recently taken a pair of scissors to her head and cut off too much hair to salvage her look. Those perpetually furrowed eyebrows, her tense lips, *what made you so unhappy Violet?* The small puncture wound above her forehead, I keep picturing the scissors, tips first, sharp enough to slice her youthful skin, *but you can't die from a bad haircut, can you?* Her mother unclasps the pearls around Violet's neck and secures them to her own. Her father pays me extra to remove the "forehead thing" from the final photograph. As he opens his suit jacket I glimpse a leather holster hugging the side of his dress shirt. They leave before the winter sun rises. Violet, dressed in polka dots.

aaron

This year, an unusually hot summer. Aaron leans on a cushioned armchair in the living room, his body bends easily and the neighbour from B6 tells me his bones shattered in several places. All the apartment windows closed mid-July. The parents, the grandparents, aunt Joanna, Lida from C2, Kasia from B5, all crammed into the kitchen, bent over the table, whispering, "...grated flesh," I set up the camera, "...stained pavement." His entire head bandaged, white gauze wrapped around and around until nothing peeks through. Nobody can tell me why they want a picture of a cloth ball with limbs. He learned to climb, first, by pulling himself up onto the couch. His next climb was onto a chair, which he used to reach a shelf, and then onto a windowsill. His head peered through the open eighth story window, he stretched out his arms, laughed at the air against his cheek, his face met cement. For the photograph they layer a grey suit overtop the clothes he wore when he fell, unwilling to peel the fabric from the skin.

charlotte

Her mother let her play in the park across the street from her house alone, watching through the window while she washed the dishes. Charlotte sat on the swings for hours, kicking her legs out into the sky, folding in her knees, again and again, a lacy pendulum. When we get to the park, me with my Brownie folding camera and Charlotte in her white coffin, three children play. Charlotte wears a full pink skirt and white lacquer shoes. Her father hoists her up onto the swing, crouches behind her, his right hand on her back, left holding her head upright. Hands unable to grasp the chains, so we tie them with cooking twine, run it through her sleeves and up the back of her jacket. I wait for the wind to die down before taking the photograph.

tessa

Apples were Tessa's favourite. She ate them sprinkled with cinnamon, sometimes in the mornings, sometimes as a treat before bed. Two-year-old Tessa, constantly chasing her brothers in the backyard, digging holes with spoons she slipped from the dinner table, the bottoms of her dresses needing re-hemming every half week. Cinnamon sprinkled apple, the only enticing object to lure her inside. Quarter past twelve the grocer delivers a bushel of apples to the studio, marked as market's best—Grimes Golden and McIntosh– *for Tessa, love always, dad*. A selection for her coffin, props for her photo shoot, I sneak myself a York Imperial for lunch, slowly twist the stem, a... b... c... d... e... f it snaps. F. Frederica... Frida... Fever. Tessa's ran scarlet, pretty common in my work. The bell above the studio door rings, "...an apple will rot, how could you even suggest..." The door swings closed behind the couple, her mother pushes a doll into my hands, pristine and porcelain, "this, I want this in the photograph." I don't mention the apples, or the picture I already took.

margot&margret

Her mother, first seeing the doll during a shopping trip, and thinking Margret had somehow crawled onto the shop's counter, turned around so frantically that her heel caught a groove in the hardwood. The hurried rotation of her hips knocked little Margret to the floor. Margot was her consolation; the two became inseparable. Two weeks later, when Margret burned her hand on the kettle, so did Margot. Seven months later, when Margret contracted the fever, so did Margot. Sore throat and soaring temperature, the rash first spreading up Margret's neck, creeping onto her cheeks, and then on to Margot's, or possibly the other way around. All over in a week and two days. Those porcelain cheeks, painted with Margret's mother's rouge, still staining Margot's face when I take the picture. Margret, pale and waxy.

nicole

Spread out on the dining table when I walk in. Her
arms flat at her sides, dressed in pants and a white
dress shirt. Her blonde, curly, shoulder-length
hair spread out on the table, stray strands stuck
between her eyelashes, tucked between her lips
and two plates. Her mother greets me at the door
with a fistful of cutlery, three Yorkshire terriers
winding in and out of her legs. "You've made it in
time for dinner," she ushers me inside, arranges
the silverware, brings out bowls with pork chops
and potatoes, piles them onto my plate. The dogs
rest their snouts against my toes and cry quietly
for leftovers. I sit in front of Nicole's nose, a metre
away from my own, shoulder to shoulder with her
mother and we eat. To my left, the curtain rises and
falls with each gust of wind and outside the window
a bird whistles, a neighbour shuts a door. Under
the table a dog's nails tap against the hardwood,
and my jaw clicks when I chew on the right side of
my mouth. I pile potatoes onto my fork, my knife
scraping against the plate; the tines accidentally
tap my teeth. Her mother eats with one hand, the

other resting on top of her daughter's. After dinner she clears the table and I set up my new, imported Butcher's Carbine.

lucy&buddy

Her father wouldn't let me take Lucy right away. I advised her parents that every minute coaxed the body further into putrescence and decay, that in a day, two days, a delicate body like Lucy's would dissolve and be unmanageable. "We're not ready. Buddy isn't ready," her mother's lips quivered. So they kept her, face up, in a sty filled with ice. Buddy didn't come home from the taxidermist for four days, and it took another to set up the shot. The blood beginning to pool on Lucy's arms, a deep purple bruise under her chin, her feet and back completely livid. Buddy, however, a piece of art— the open mouth, curious eyes—about to lick his mistress's hand, one paw raised as if he was tugging on her dress, *come play*. Lucy, liquefied limbs and extinction scented, surrounded by her ball, flowers, best friend. Before leaving I make sure to ask for the taxidermist's name and city.

grace&nancy

I make Grace&Nancy hold up Grace&Nancy for the shot. I don't remember which is which, but my subject's the one on the right. Their father brings them in one September morning, surging through the swinging door, nonchalantly scraping his soles against the threshold before herding his daughters—one hand on his live daughter's neck, the dead daughter squeezed between his chest and forearm—in front of my current backdrop, pale blue with a tinge of apricot. The family's been meaning to take this picture for a while, but then Grace&Nancy got sick, so better late. "Actually, I told their mother I left the photo at the office," he lets slip, "she doesn't know I'm here." At first we have trouble keeping Grace&Nancy's head up, her neck slouches to her chin and Grace&Nancy's arms tire. We decide to use a stand, secured behind and around Grace&Nancy's neck, and I paint on her eyes, which I later carefully dissolve with some olive oil before her father slips her into the backseat of the carriage like a plank of wood.

jesse&jonah

Their mother leaves the room while I take the photograph. Jesse&Jonah, three months and two days, joined from the breastbone to the bellybutton, two distinct cries, but only one heartbeat. I hear the oven door open, slam shut. A squirrel scrabbles across the roof. Their twin older brothers play with blocks in the pantry. Jesse&Jonah rest their heads against each other's, strands of thin brown hair intertwined. A wooden bowl clatters onto the floor, the swish of a broom. Posed on their parents' bed, their body the same size as the crushed velvet throw pillows that pad them on either end. Four cramped scraggly arms and two feet peeking through a satin gown, twenty fingers and ten toes. I slip out the back door of the kitchen; no mother baking pies, no children plotting in the corner.

meta&mida&minta

Their aunt floats around them, delicately lifting up their arms with her thumb and forefinger. She arranges their hands, first straight at their sides, then gently across their bellies. She tilts their heads, Meta to the right, Minta to the left, and takes care to balance Mida's head so it doesn't lean too much to either shoulder. She combs her fingers through the organza, blending their gowns together, tucking the fabrics underneath each other until they merge into one cohesive sheet. Their mother watching from her bed on the other side of the room, her own body buried in blankets up to her neck, four fingertips hanging off the side of the mattress facing the triplets, faintly trembling. Throughout my shoot, I can hear her mumbling... mine   mine   mine

27

timothy&eliza

Two bodies, one bed. Timothy&Eliza wear matching cream-coloured gowns, small pleats across their chest. I shoot them from the waist up. Tim, a year old when he contracted the chicken pox. Quarantined too late, it spread to his sister, eleven-year-old Eliza, destroying her life, too. I position Eliza's arms; arrange her left fingers across her right hand. Timothy's arms still too short to cross comfortably so I rest his wrists parallel. The wall behind them covered in ornate wallpaper, tea coloured with green and purple flourishes. Their mother holds out an embossed copper photo mat, asks if she can order a picture that "fits this" since it "matches the wallpaper." Sixth-plate tintype, I nod and make a note.

renée

The family gathers into the living room: mother, father, a boy of about ten, and his four younger sisters. The smallest, Renée, born and died two months premature, is laid out on a table in her baptismal gown, the only dress that was ever exclusively her own. Like her sisters, she would have worn hand-me-downs. White netting hangs from a raised stand, drapes over her body and around the bouquets of carnations surrounding her, some carnations larger than Renée's head. The family sits, three on each side. Two large prints of both sets of grandparents hang framed on the purple and gold patterned wallpaper. Just as I take the picture, the youngest living daughter squirms out of her father's lap, disturbing the symmetry. Her face blurred in the photograph.

lily

The garden bursts and blooms, the air smells like nectar and flesh. Guests eat biscuits and sip tea around the lawn, women in woven floppy hats, flowers pinned to their rims, men in light linen shirts. Rows of roses and gardenias line the fence and in the north corner grows a small orchard of apples. One of her sisters and two of her brothers chuck fallen apples back and forth, use each other's backs as stepstools and pick the fresh ones, sink their teeth into sour peels. Strings lined with small paper ornaments strung across the yard, from the roof to the back fence near Lily, laid out in a sundress, white with red polka dots. The afternoon hot and sweat pools underneath my necktie, soaks through my tunic. Lily, outside since before I arrived. Her white painted coffin rests in a trough of ice underneath an oversized parasol. A crown of silver cosmos around her head.

victoria

They sit, stoic. The father runs his fingers through his hair, adjusts his bowtie. His overcoat dark chestnut, same as the coffin wood. He carried it himself, cradled it for blocks, resting his cheek against the lid, up two streets and down three to my studio. The bones rattling inside the body rattling inside the box, all shaking to his step, his palms. Two streams of tears down his beard. I set up some upholstered chairs and he props the coffin forty-five degrees to the camera, slips off the lid and hands it to me. I rest it against the coffin's right side, to add a dark line to the right edge of the shot, but I don't tell the father that. He sags down onto a chair as I ruffle the blanket around the baby, pull its hands out and position them centre. He holds a handkerchief in one hand; his other hand rests defeated, his knuckles bumping against the casket, his fingernails tapping the chair's edge.

kacper

I take the photo while on the road. A funeral procession into a small church, a pinebox half the size of the men carrying it, I slip inside the door, "photograph?" Two men carry the boy towards me. His body slides loosely inside the coffin, a soft *thunk* when his head taps the upper panel. The coffin just a few inches too big, or maybe his body too dehydrated. A few days decay has flattened his fingers. I borrow a cloth tarp from the church basement and the men prop him up on a shipping container—FOR ALL COOKING SNOWDRIFT PERFECT SHORTENING—they wedge a hammer between the two boxes, angle the boy for my shot. His body skates down, his feet sink into the corners, his ankles curl. Socks cover his legs above the knees, which must be black with blood pooled against the surface.

harold

I take a photograph of Harold's miniature casket interior upholstered with white satin, adorned with ruches and bows. Harold lies on a flattened pillow lined with scallops of snowy organza. He blends in: a white gown, thick cotton tights, and a delicate silver cross upon his chest. His grandmother kept a can under the stove to catch the leaking coal oil. Since learning to crawl, he opened all the floor cupboards; pulled the pots and steel frying pans onto the floor, knocked them against each other. He crawled across the kitchen tiles, laughing, giggling, baby talking. And then he was quiet. Harold quiet. His grandmother, preparing dinner at the counter, noticed the silence right away too late. Enough time to hear the faint squeak of the rolling pin as it scraped across the dough. She found him sitting in front of the stove, the tin can between his palms, the kerosene dribbling down from the corners of his mouth and onto his chin. The black fluid already deep in his system, coating his esophagus, lining his stomach walls, absorbing into his bloodstream.

reese

From the cottage we walk in procession. Reese's mother and father pallbear her pinebox through the front door, and I follow with my camera. Between the trees grass and foliage, a worn, narrow path leads us to a private beach and a fishing dock. Reese spent hours on the dock with her father; catching sunfish with rods he made for her out of tree branches and twine. Damp sand finds its way into my loafers. Her parents march the coffin to the end of the dock, set it down and lift the lid. Reese wears a simple violet dress with a black satin sash. A mosquito lands under my eye, takes a drink. Two days ago Reese wandered out alone, long after midnight, hung her feet off the edge of the dock, counted the shadows of fish swimming by, leaned in too close. Her mother found her floating face down, her body bumping the canoe with each wave, *thump thump.*

darkroom

Unpin your children from the twine. Spread across the table. Pick her out from the collection, the contrast of her lace dress to the texture of the cushions, the way you interlaced her stiff fingers and angled her nose. Curl each corner, tuck. The rest you fold between sheets of tissue and pile into another box. The box you pile with the other boxes. Some people collect coins. Sometimes you wake up and hope for tragedy. You fill boxes, they fill coffins. Do they notice the burn, dodge—the composition of each centred body. Do they know which direction a pupil faces even when the eyes are closed? And what will you look like draped over a couch, will your hair be grey? Who will dip swish and tuck you into their portfolio? They're starting to print your work in magazines.

vanya

Vanya comes into the studio the afternoon after his christening, his hair still damp. His mother brought him a week earlier, but each time I focused the camera Vanya would scream, his neck twist, and I'd hesitate over the capture button, sure the photo would produce a demon not a baby. I told his mother and she left, only to come back "while the devil's out and the holy spirit's fresh." She lifts him out of his stroller, bounces him in her arms, "Vanya will behave today, he's wearing the same baptismal robe all my children wore..." I sit his mother in a chair, drape her with a sheet of black satin, arrange Vayna on her lap, her voice muffled, "...I've seen your pictures, you make children look divine..." Dead children. Who don't blink or cry. Don't complain that their noses are cold or their arms stiff. "And make sure you get the entire robe, especially the crochet detail at the bottom," dead babies don't have bad photos, "...I'm sending this picture to my sister back in the Ukraine..." no re-dos, "...Vanya's such an angel..." at least today he looks dead enough.

part II

obituaries

eugene

Eugene will be right in. His wife Clara flicks the light switch on her way inside the house and his next step triggers a deluge of light from atop the rising garage door. He shuffles into a dirty lawn chair, coated in car exhaust, at the mouth of their driveway. Ash, dust, the garage air a blend of oil, wood, and soil. Forty years of machinery hang against the walls,

garden tools	tucked atop the
rafters. This	summer Clara
will find the	crumpled LCBO
bags he	hid behind the
cupboards,	s e c r e t
insulation,	more stashed
atop the	b a s e m e n t ' s
ceiling tiles.	Last summer
they sat out	here, dragging

their chairs between the shade and sunshine, a pitcher of water resting on the car trunk. The garage light barely spreads past the edge of the house, greyscaling across the pavement until it reaches blackness just past the corner of orange bricks. The driveway extends for a couple metres more, up ahead it crosses the sidewalk and blends out into the road, but he can't see that far. November nuzzles up against his skin, stiffens his joints, his neck tenses against the cold plastic. The house to his right, Clara inside slipping into her nightgown, folding the bed cover into a neat rectangle and stacking it on the dresser with the embroidered pillows; the same routine every night. On the left, his neighbours' house, a shrub and flower garden running between the wall and his driveway. In two years the neighbours will sell the house and the new owner will rip out the flowers and vines and bushes, even the roses because they look like weeds. She will bleach the grass with pesticide on both sides of the chain-link fence to kill off all the roots and cover the remaining soil with smooth, grey garden stones. He inhales November. Chicha the cat pokes her head into the light of the driveway. In four years she'll find herself on this driveway for the last time, her stomach flat, spilling out, the pavement damp with blood and intestinal fluid, dragged up from the road; she won't make it to the front door. Clara will make sure to bury Chicha in the backyard, by the old tomato garden. He sinks lower into his lawn chair, outside just over five minutes. Twenty minutes ago leaving his sister-in-law's house. In three minutes Clara will step outside in her nightgown, ask him what he thinks he's still doing, tell him to get inside and go to sleep. The garage light will go on as she opens the back door. In ten minutes the ambulance will leave the driveway without turning on the sirens.

four years from now your
neighbours' neighbour's
house catches fire twice,
once by accident, once
because he didn't know
what to do with the body
dragging from the bed to the
kitchen to the fire hydrant
across your driveway

helena

Helena's been in bed for seven weeks, a skeleton. Hedwig tries to make her eat, at least drink something. Someone is always in her room, watching her, watching her watch *The Bold and the Beautiful*. Hedwig, Stan, Karoline, Hedwig, Stan, sometimes Marcin her grandson, sometimes Marcin her grandson in-law. Two summers ago she watched Karoline get married in the new church they built on the edge of town, skipped going to the reception, the wedding the last time she stepped out the front gate. A

gave her
before
over to
last rites.
then, but
bedsheets
w a t e r .
she's had

week ago Hedwig
a sponge bath
the priest came
administer her
Helena, ready
still here, her
smell of holy
Every physical
tells her she's in

great shape, but every few months it's a new joint or a new muscle—still great for 93, Hedwig tells her, as great as 93 can be. At night she's awake and waiting. Dear Lord, why haven't you taken me yet? I'm ready Lord, just take me already. Tomorrow Karoline will brush her hair; they'll watch *The Bold and the Beautiful*. She'll ask Stan to read her a passage from one of his romance novels. He'll read her a passage about the protagonist missing her lover. Two days from now she'll look around at her parlour bedroom, a couch, glass coffee table, bed, TV, she'll say goodbye for the –undreth time. She'll say goodbye to the quilt Hedwig bought her at the new shopping complex, to the curtains that have been greeting her every morning for the last 10 of the 30 years she's lived with Hedwig and Stan. She'll find a new scratch on the wall next to her nose to say goodbye to. She'll ask Karoline to leave the closet door open so she can say goodbye to the little pink granny sweater her grandson Paul sent her from London, Canada, hope they don't bury her in that. Goodbye to the tie-at-the-neck secretary blouses she wore in the 70s, trendy again 33 years later, good thing she kept them. Three days from now she'll eat two spoons of Hedwig's chicken noodle soup, the tin can taste both repulsive and nostalgic. Stan will read her the new garden pruning article he wrote for the town newspaper. Libús the dog will run in the room and she'll scowl at him in her head. The cat will bat her tail from the window in the evening. Midnight, Hedwig, Stan, Karoline, Marcin&Marcin will be in her room. False alarm, back in bed by 1. Back around her bed at 3, Hedwig with her under the sheets.

when *the bold and the beautiful* first aired, 1994 poland, seven years after the usa, at least 6000 episodes deep now so entwined with the day-to-day behind the glass screen the show will go on even when your contract expires

walter

Walter stands up, four in the morning, he can barely make himself out in the vanity mirror. Stella opens her eyes, always acutely aware of him in relation to her, what angle, how many metres. The bedroom feels foreign, like waking up in a hotel halfway across the ocean. The bed, the vanity, television static behind every eyelid hovers around him. The room lit pale navy. A decade ago his daughter held sleepovers in a tent she set up in the backyard. The girls would sneak out after midnight. Sometimes he'd stand behind the curtain until he heard the gate click shut, the tent zip closed. That's why he's awake now? May and his daughter in her twenties, she hasn't sneaked out in years. "Are you okay?" "I'm fine," he says and collapses. Maybe it's 210 pounds hitting the floor in the room next door, or maybe it's her mother's shriek, his daughter jolts out of her dream and runs. No fire, no wire, obviously not, but 13 years of swimming floods into her mind, soaks her skull, clogs her ear canals. Hands over his chest, 30 compressions. Her mother stumbling into her slippers to call an ambulance. No fire, no wire, no gas, no glass. Chin up, plug nose, two breaths. Fire, wire, gas, glass, pump, pump, pump, breathe, breathe. Fire, wire, wireless. Internet. Dad didn't let her have the Internet in the house until high school; she spent her afternoons in the library trying to catch up with

the world for   a maximum
two hours at   the terminal
per day. The   year was
2004. Fire,   pump, pump,
wire, breath,   breath. Gas.
Glass. Dad   stores his
e x t e n s i v e   collection of
bottles in the   b a s e m e n t
bar. Glass   cat bottles of

wine, sampled sized glass bottles of liquor. For her birthday parties he mixed mock cocktails until she was 17. Pump, breathe. She holds her breath while she pumps. Pump, breathe, mustache in her mouth. Pump, pump, jump on one leg and shake her head in the opposite direction to get the water out. Pump.

her butterfly stroke from the
bleachers, chlorine lungs and
orange swim caps, scallop
through the water faster fast-
er faster her bedroom walls
ribbon lined—first place!—
here and for you

libuś

Libuś is the king of the neighbourhood. He knows this because he never has to wear a leash when Stan takes him out for a walk. He roams where he wants to roam, but mostly they tread down the block, up 4th Street, around the fishing pond at Green Park. Sometimes he'll get a few stick throws into the water. He makes sure to mark the trees on the way, and the fence post, and the garbage bins. He saves his pee all day for these evening walks, rationing out enough to cover all his territory, he is king. Sometimes it's not enough, but he'll still do the hind leg raise on all the usual spots, for show to other dogs, local or visiting. Sometimes he'll break away from Stan, refuse to

walk back	home, stay a
day at the	park, in the
f o r e s t ,	maybe go
down to	town, chase
the lady	dogs. Stan
will go	home, watch
the evening	news, leave
the gate	open and
stay up just	a bit later to

open the door when Libuś shows up barking after dark. Tonight he doesn't bark, but he's managed to drag himself up the stairs onto the porch, smearing blood on the yellow steps, Stan already asleep. It'll be a dry burgundy when Stan finds him in the morning, clumped in the fur around his neck where his flesh separates from the muscle underneath. Four years ago, in the summer, Stan's son Paul thought it would be funny to tie a baby bib around Libuś's neck; it was their daughter's, Stan's first granddaughter, and he'd kept it all these years in a drawer with his own children's mementos. They laughed until Libuś escaped from the front gate and came back two hours later sans bib. No luck with his neck. Five months from now, Stan will adopt a new dog, Maya, a short-legged Corgi who won't run as fast as Libuś but will have to wear a leash on walks. In two years she'll escape her leash for less than two hours and return pregnant. They'll name one of the puppies Libuś, but they'll give it away and who knows what doggie name the new owners will choose: Rufus? Buddy? King?

you crank your neck when you
hear *na spacer*, ready to run,
feed ticks with your blood,
paws against pavement,
grass, dirt, a branch to throw
catch throw keep away mutt
smell in the air makes you
wild chase

ella

It started with her ear, just a bump, an itch. She
scratched until it scabbed over. When her daughter
was seven a colony of bees moved into the walls of
their basement living room. For several months they
w e n t   unnoticed,
pollinating   her garden,
l a y i n g   eggs   and
hatching in-   between the
p l y w o o d .   First   she
s t a r t e d   finding dead
bees on the   carpet,   in
her laundry,   and then the
humming of   thousands of
wings beating against the wooden panels, first a low
vibration—she told herself it was just in her head—
escalated to a consistent murmur and then: Bees
started to burst out, pushing their way out of the
drop ceiling tiles, falling on the coffee table while
she smoked, pulsing in the bathroom vanity. She
called her brother and a beekeeper and the three of
them removed the panels, the bees crawling from
the walls, expanding like out of a clown car. The

beekeeper gassed them, plucked out the queen, and drove them to his honey farm. She changes the gauze around her ear twice daily, cleaning the pus and blood. Two summers ago, when her daughter left for university, a woodpecker took a liking to the decorative cedar panels outside the house, continuously pecking at the same hole every morning, *peck, peck,* her alarm clock. Radiation seemingly killed the bump, but as soon as her hair grew back two inches she felt a familiar itch underneath her skin. Her daughter took a semester off from school. Last autumn a squirrel found a hole in the roof and squeezed its way inside to build a nest. As the spring approached she could hear the *patter patter* across the ceiling overtop the living room. She sits in her armchair and follows the noise with her neck. The bump consumes her, eats her from the inside, nestled inside her body, sucking her skin tight against her bones.

cat paws swat your face
early morning birds warble
when the sun rises go outside
car alarm down the street,
neighbour's   dog   howls
through the fence,   each
footstep slaps ground vibrate
through your spine ear
scratch listen scratch scratch

bogdan

Saturday night and the kids are out. Bogdan's at home with the three boys, because that's what grandpas do. Sebastian and Nick, upstairs playing computer games in their bedrooms, one hand cemented to their mice, the other hand swapping between a can of coke and the keyboard. Grandpa downstairs with Jacob, watching *X-Men* on pay-per-view. Jake dressed as a cross between Indiana Jones—whip—and Rambo—knife and headband. Toys litter the floor, mostly army men and dinosaurs engaged in a full-on war, monster versus machine. Two weeks from now Bogdan leaves on the annual fishing trip he takes with his son-in-law. He'll have to organize his fishing tackle this week. The cabbage rolls his wife made tucked away in the basement freezer. He won't get a taste. The movie background noise against the lake water of Northern Ontario, the smell of gutted fish. He fed the boys some Hawaiian pizza before the movie, Nick and Sebastian disappearing up the stairs with their plates. The way the dragonflies swoop around the dock in the evening, his beer and his fishing rod. Four months from now his prediction will come true, his first granddaughter born on a Tuesday afternoon. He'll never get to meet her, but she'll wear his crooked nose. The noise of the boat smacking the water when it comes up against a wave. In two days his brother-in-law's brother motionless and cold in his bed, two funerals in two days, and all that paperwork. Hooking a fat worm through the head, then looping it around and hooking it in the middle for extra hold. When the movie ends Jake runs up stairs to tell his brothers that grandpa, "won't wake up to change the channel."

retired from the foundry
since the first heart attack
babysitting you as much as
you babysit them the kid's
kids grow up so seven years
from now there's nine, three
you'll never meet

sasha

Since the knee surgery Sasha prefers to shower downstairs. Seated on a taupe perforated bench, which arrived with his mother-in-law, he adjusts the heat, lets the water flow over his head, dribble onto his lap. Ramona applies foundation in front of her vanity, smoothing out her skin, smoothing out her skin, upstairs in the real house. The real house, a nickname from when they first moved in. The plan was to section off the downstairs and rent it out to young couples that, like them, had moved to the city to work in the automotive field. But this was before illness hit Ramona's mother particularly hard

one winter and she	m o v e d
in downstairs. Two	y e a r s
later her cat went	b l i n d
and she reasoned	that to
move away would	disorient
him. When the	c a t
wandered a bit too	far from
the sidewalk she	w e p t

loudly, Sasha and Ramona could hear her at night with their door closed, and by then she didn't have many years left either, though, in line with her stubborn nature, she held on for another fourteen. He thinks about her every time he showers in her shower. He leans forward; the water slides down his back. He leans back, lifting one leg at a time, letting the stream dribble down around his ankles. He continues to move his body under the stream like this, fighting his stiff tendons, trying to spread the heat evenly across himself, his body cooling faster than the water can warm him. Ramona putting on her perfume—Estée Lauder Youth Dew—the scent the same one she's worn for thirty-one years. He forgets what her skin smelled like when they were still young. Estée now penetrates the bedsheets, the living room furniture; he smells her when he opens the garage door. Tonight, dinner at his sister-in-law's. An hour later the water still runs, completely cold, creeping up against the edges of the shower, sloshing gently onto the tile floor, a narrow stream trickling through the door into the basement drain. Ramona upstairs asleep in the living room armchair, the morning news muted on the television. The decaf coffee she made him lukewarm on the counter.

down six and eight stairs
to get to her domain even
though she's been gone eleven
years her reading glasses rest
on the table top magazines
tucked under the coffee you
recycle sears fliers with her
name every three months

alan

He kicks his feet into the air, toes pointed as he swoops, bends his knees for the return, up and back, the swing chains rusty. He dreamed of the emptiness. Of getting away from early mornings and the car assembly line. Of sitting out on the lake in his motorboat, line and lure. He bought the cottage because of the high ceilings and the almost five kilometres of gravel crunching under his tires from the main road to his driveway. When the sun sets he lights a campfire and strums acoustic melodies that echo off into the distant trees. It's been three years and his friends drove up to visit once. They drank moonshine from sunrise and fished until evening, pan-fried fresh sea bass for dinner. They returned to their families with coolers filled with fillets and wild mushrooms. He returns to the campfire and the constellations, waves "hi Orion" in the sharp March air. White knuckles and legs outstretched—

swing up and back—the tight squeak of swaying chain links. Since moving in he's witnessed the trees grow an inch, the shoreline erode a few millimetres, the grass overtake the driveway, poke through the sidewalk crevices, and engulf the yard in white clover and dandelion - except the patch beneath the swing where his heels grip the dirt. Up and back. Sometimes he can hear laughter from across the lake, the distant bass line of a summer party, cannon balls into the water. Up and back. When they find him he's stopped swinging. Un-loop the belt from the closet rod, a pile of sweaters toppled over, his socks drooping from his toes.

six in the morning still water
putput through the fog, pull
back and cast, the line whim-
pers water gently ripples and
you reel and reel back across
the gravel and the highway to
six-day workweeks and day-
dreaming the lake's lullaby

derrick

He starts and ends his day on the porch. A Heineken before noon. He gets up at 9:15 to weed the lawn. By brunch he's watched two new dandelion buds spread out their petals and face the sun. He retired from the Chrysler assembly line seven years ago. Clears his throat and gulps. He makes a list of the unfinished things: painting the drywall in the attic, putting doors on the cabinets, opening the pool, those goddamn half cars. He starts in the backyard, rests his elbows on the edge of the above-ground pool. A cherry falls from the tree behind him and he picks it up, pops it inside his mouth, spits out the pit. Drains the pool of black water and algae that's gathered over the winter. The memory of a timid voice behind

him   asks,   "When   can
we   swim?"   His   wife
used   to   b a b y s i t .
He'll run a   hose   down
the driveway   so the water
f l o w s   against   the
curb   and   into   the
sewer.   He   used to show

the kids how to make folded paper boats to race down the stream. The backyard littered with half cars covered with tarps. One day he will Frankenstein them into something that runs. But by the afternoon, four beers deep, picks a dandelion puff, makes a wish and in one breath blows the seeds across his neighbour's driveway. In the kitchen the cabinets sit door-less, his wife could only take two years of exposed plates and mugs before she left. He opens the fridge and grabs a beer. A steak in the freezer for tonight's dinner, he'll have to clean the grill, adds it to his list of unfinished things, and microwaves yesterday's spaghetti. Maybe sell the house? Back on the porch by five, when his neighbours come home from work, waving at them as the remote control locks on their cars *beepbeep* and they duck into their houses. As the sun sets he settles into his bed in the attic, turns on the television. The sound of the comedy channel echoes against the unpainted drywall and into his dreams. It plays throughout the next morning, the whole week. The front lawn a jungle of gold and green. The unpainted attic, the un-doored cabinets, the undrained pool, the uncovered cars, the unscraped barbecue.

pile firewood from your trunk
to front lawn your neighbours'
backyards bring drinks your
lonely porch talk global weath-
er talk city politics relish the
last few weeks of temperate
breeze retreat to your living
room desolate winter in the
un-house

vivian

The blood pressure machine's constant *beep beep beeping*, a barely noticeable rhythm as Vivian checks her blood pressure once, twice, at least four times in a row. Pulls up a chart on her computer screen where she tracks her progress, writes today's average, one-oh-eight over seventy-two. There's a small lump growing on   the side of
her tongue   that   she
diagnoses   as   not   a
canker   sore so she
rinses   her   mouth with
dentist   prescribed
Peridex   e   v   e   r   y
night.   Sits at the
computer,   typing   in
her symptoms—sweating, itchy forearms, veiny eyes—grouping and combining them until something emergency worthy piques her interest. She has her doctor's secretary on speed dial, number 4 after her husband and two daughters. She's drafted a catalogue of safety rules: before her daughters get in the driver's seat she repeats, "drive slowly, check

your blind spots, pay attention to other drivers." When they go dancing on the weekend, "never put your drink down, go to the bathroom in twos." Before sleepovers when they were young, "don't burn candles." Before leaving them home alone, "don't forget to turn the stove off. Don't open the door for strangers. If someone calls and you don't recognize the voice, tell him or her I'm busy... And don't jump, don't ever jump." When her daughters were in primary school she drove past the playground in the winter to make sure the kids weren't outside for recess when the wind chill was too high. So afraid of accidents, so afraid of dying. She has come close twice, once when she lost her footing in the shallow end of a public pool before learning to swim, and once in a car accident. She was driving, her daughter, three years old in the back seat, when the car behind them collided into their back bumper and sandwiched them between a semi. When she was nine her mother almost died during childbirth, forty-six years she lives twenty houses down the street and comes over on weekends for orange pekoe.

beep beep your blood pressure and check check the wall outlets unplug unnecessary electronics and check check that the lights are off get in the car get out of the car to double check check that the door is locked check

part III

skin graft

7 stages

1. colours abandon your face
2. chill until room temperature
3. rigor mortis
4. blood rush pulls your bruises to the surface
   pools beneath your thin skin mauve
5. organs boil, churn paste from your abscess
   acidic delicious you swell up and ooze from
   the orifices
6. unwrite your history and wilt into simple
   matter, feed plants with your nutrients
   destroy, confine, position, erase any
   semblance of your face and leave behind
   your scaffolding
7. find you at a dig site, brush the dust from
   your bones, fine frail, piece you like a puzzle,
   build you from your toes to your skull,
   speculate about the colour of your hair, how
   many sugars you like in your tea

gossamer

Post-mortem pale. She taught herself how to swim when she was thirteen so she wouldn't have to wear lifejackets in Michelle's backyard pool. They would float away the afternoon, eat dinner, swim until sunset. In the water, the colour of her lips faded from a neutral pink to bruised blue, matching the pool liner. That same blue, now the colour of her apartment throw cushions, the mug she drinks her morning hot chocolate from, the box holding her eyeglasses, and the highlighter ink throughout her notes. All the adults commented on her lips, the onset of hypothermia, and how she needed to get out of the water right this moment. When she turned sixteen she started wearing Vegas Volt lipstick, a bright creamy orange in a sleek black bullet tube. Her complexion always the lightest shade of foundation available. Pale peach, ballet pink, eggshell, transparent. Michelle used to tease that her face was transparent—the layers of skin underneath her eyes so thin her veins showed. "Are you feeling okay?" Her mother could always tell when a migraine loomed. Her face drained after tap class, she couldn't take the noise of the shuffle hops, ball changes, the metal against wood of twenty other feet. Her head pulsing in tune to the recital music. She had to drop tap lessons and only danced in soft shoes, ballet and jazz. Her face never cooperates. The slightest blush flushes her cheekbones scarlet, stress from upcoming exams breaks out her chin and forehead. She's tried a few brands of foundation, learned to mix it with a heavy duty concealer, it's hard to erase the dead girl look from her face, her sunken eyes, the way her hands always radiate cold.

.

the whale

Pieces of blue whale rain from the sky. Blood and fat and digested krill scatter the beach, chunks fly far above the sand dunes, land on parked cars and break windshields. Brine and burnt skin, slightly fishy. Technicians, reporters, and city officials dart beneath the fleshy hail, throw their arms above their heads, shield their eyes, their jackets smeared with drops of liquefied whale, meat in their hair.

The whale washed up on shore early Sunday morning. Its body stretched across the beach, 26 metres long and two people tall. Died out in the ocean, the waves gently rocking it from the depths to the sand. The sun rose and the salt water beat against its back until the whale had lodged itself securely on the shore. By Monday, families filled the usually empty November parking lots. Parents posed their children with the creature. By Tuesday the city had blocked off the beach. They stuffed the whale with dynamite, confident that the blast would disintegrate the giant, dissolve its decomposing body, clean it from the shore. Cheap and easy.

gooseflesh

Mid January, many degrees below zero, dry air, high winds, pajama pants. Locked out of her house, not the first time, but never in this weather and in this outfit. She heard the crash, slipped on some shoes, her jacket, grabbed her camera. Neighbours already outside, rushing to the mangled car with blankets, calling 911, neighbours she's never seen before accumulating in the middle of the road. She stands on the edge of her porch, takes a few pictures to show her parents, one of the glass scattered on the road, a close-up of the dented SUV and the broken fence, she walks back to the door... No hat, no gloves. The wind ignoring the fabric of her pajama pants, slapping her legs dry. The sirens getting closer. Her hands still holding the camera, red and dry, she takes another picture of emergency vehicles. Her neighbours excitedly chatting in the street, taking long drags from their cigarettes, drinking coffee from ceramic mugs. Her ears numb. A man removed from the front seat of the first vehicle, declines the stretcher, limps towards the ambulance. The other car already empty, the owner speaking to the police. A trembling snapshot.

archaeology

Bones beneath damp sand, and soil that when squeezed between her palms, falls apart when she reopens. Stray grains of sand lodged in the crumbling skeleton pores. Bones, just large enough for a small child. Two ribs, a femur. A day of rain and heavy wind unearths the sandbox cellar, over in the far corner of the park, near the benches where the parents sit, where children won't play in case their parents call "we're going home." She's a 4-year-old archaeologist, digging to the other side of the earth. She finds a dinosaur. Keeps a bone, slips it into her pocket to bring home and stash in a shoebox below her bed.

cremation

On the mantle a miniature vessel, a jar, created with cheap ceramic and acrylic paint. A teardrop-shaped bowl, a lid with a knob. No cookies inside, just crumbs. More fine than crumbly. Ashy powder. Twirl a fingertip inside, the ashes coat your prints, snuggle under your nails. Taste what remains. Smear across your forehead. From ash you were born, to cookies you will return. Two and a half cups of flowers by the grave. Pinch of salt, tons of butter. Chocolate chips.

bruises

Her first ones she doesn't remember, she only remembers the kisses. Then there was the bruise from standing at the bottom of the hill while the boy on the bike rode down. They tumbled; bike, boy, her, boy, bike, grass. Her arm bruised from her elbow up to her shoulder. Multiple bruises from hitting corners of doorways, doorknobs, end tables. She inherited clumsiness from her mother. The completely inexplicable bruises: the bruise on her pinky finger, the bruise above her eyebrow, the bruise behind her ear, the bruise on the side of her neck—or was that one a hickey? The bruise in the shape of an elephant on her left thigh. With a trunk, tusks, one big floppy ear. She used a pen to fill in the smaller details—an eye, long eyelashes—she wore dresses, lifted up their hems, performed the bruise until it faded. Then the bruise she got in the bar on Hallowe'en from tripping when her wizard cape caught underneath the stool. That bruise gripped her leg well into the Christmas season, gravity pulling the blood in her body, drooping from mid-calf to below her ankle, a tapestry of purple and rust and week-old banana. The winter also brought annual bruised butt cheeks, miscalculating the placement of the ice on the sidewalk on her walk to the bus stop in the morning. Heat, rising through the apartment floor, colliding with her puddled blood.

taxidermy

Start with hind legs. Route a blade up the calf where muscle meets skin. Cut a seam up belly, fur and fat. Peel. Hook hoof to a lever on the ceiling; hoist carcass off the ground. Smoke a cigarette. Strip cadaver skin, pull south, from rump, the chest, front legs, undress the neck, smoothly. At the chin saw drop the body. Dispose. Hang the head by antlers, detach pelt from bone muscle, slit away the gums, round the eye sockets, tug with tender fingertips, don't rip. Saw off skull cap horns. Clean the coat, salt dry. Eat a tuna salad sandwich. Drill the antlers to the mount, bone to plastic with two screws. Drape hide over fake face, tuck and glue, sew shut the seam, and hang above the fireplace.

motion sickness

She's in a bathroom in Burgundy, France, kneeled over the toilet, completely letting go of lunch. She can taste quiche and quinoa, backwards from the order she ingested at breakfast, scratching her esophagus on the way up. Every summer her parents took road trips, driving across Western Ontario, her motion sickness dictating where they stopped. She always travelled with plastic bags.

The bottle of Dramamine unopened inside her suitcase back at the hotel, and even if she'd brought it, she's far too gone. She's made this mistake before. Once on a car ride from Southern California to Vegas for her 21st birthday, where she sipped tea all night because she couldn't keep the food in her stomach *before* alcohol. Once on an airplane when she was eleven, during a turbulent landing that made her so sick she actually used the plane provided barf bag from the seat pocket. Once in Disneyland on the virtual reality Star Wars ride, watching a 3D movie in a small moving room, jolting her forward, left right back, sitting with her palms closed and eyes sweating.

She fights her stomach muscles, but they beat harder and it all comes up in waves. Gags until only clear bile exits her mouth. But she still heaves and heaves, so hard, she's sure her stomach will force itself out through her mouth and land inside out on the pastel tiles, a splash of sour quinoa seeds on her chin.

composting

Playing in the dirt while her mother gardened, one of her earliest memories. She scratched the soil with a handheld rake and searched for worms inside chunks of mud. Her mother planted rows of tomatoes. Then cucumbers and beets, radishes and turnips, dill and chives and sorrel. Raspberry, blueberry, gooseberry, and currant bushes lined the back fence. Her mother took her to the garden shops and street-side greenhouses that popped up in spring. Together they walked the narrow rows of potted flowers, bought trays of sprouts and seed pouches. They'd load the car with fertilizer, soil, and red decorative wood chips for the front yard. The wood chips still there, a wine tinge underneath layers of decaying maple leaves and helicopters. The driveway empty, so she slips through the gate and into the backyard. The grass cut neat, the vegetable patch only dirt. She sits in a white plastic yard chair. In the corner, the black compost barrel. Only six when they installed it and that summer she routinely opened the lid expecting the leaves and grass to magically transform. She loved finding roly polies, poking them so they'd curl into tight balls, she'd roll them around her palm. Pill bugs reminded her mother of cemeteries, always crawling out from underneath the gravestones, snacking on the dead.

Her first boyfriend gave her two roses and a poem; one pink and the other he spray-painted black. The roses from her second boyfriend she hung upside down to dry, turned the petals into potpourri sprayed with his cologne, kept them on her desk until she moved out of her parents' house. Every weekend her chores included dusting the potted palm, gently running a wet terry cloth over each leaf careful not to cut herself on the paper-sharp foliage. For her first apartment she bought a ball cactus. Her third boyfriend never bought her flowers. Every Tuesday she buys fresh tulips at the grocery store, like her mother used to.

At her mother's grave she planted marigolds and chives.

insect suicide

A cicada repeatedly slamming into the window, its wings
  vibrating against the glass with each impact.
The smell of a moth that lands on a light bulb and burns
  off its feet.
When a hornet gets greedy for fruit juice and drowns in
  the watermelon punch.
Ants that march in tight rows from one end of the bicycle
  path to the other.
Worms that squirm out of the soil on a rainy day only to
  drown in puddles on the pavement.
Worms that survive the puddles only to fry in the sun.
Spiders that spin their webs in doorframes.
Fruit flies that fly into spider webs in doorframes.
Mantises cannibalized for sex.
Mosquitos that drink long enough to get swatted.
Midges, just because they look like mosquitos.
Botfly larva that burrow themselves into wealthy
  tourists.
Slugs that squeeze under kitchen doorframes into lines
  of salt.

Fireflies that fly into bonfires looking for a mate in the
sparks.

Caterpillars that snack on leaves sprayed with pesticide.

Fleas that choose to jump to the fur of well-groomed pets.

Butterflies that fly too close to summer camp kids with
bug catching nets.

Houseflies lured by the refrigerator's light bulbs in the
night, frozen in the morning.

Mayflies gathered under streetlamps; the crunch of
several carcasses when a car drives by.

fishbone

Tug hook. Throat flesh tears, fingers deep inside lips, wiggle rip. Cut the line and let slip into bucket, body curved around the edges. Faint flop splash and then still—pull from copper-tinged water, slap on the cutting board. Tuck knife under scales and scrape—pop pop—and stick to your sweater, decorate your hair like opal sequins. Belly slice from chin to tail. Scoop intestines with your fingers, xylophone against the hollow spine. Guillotine behind the gills, find the mangled earthworm. Rinse clean and sea salt, bathe in egg yolk. Flour and slide into sizzling oil.

warta

She takes a great gulp of cold sandy water as the river almost swallows her. She had just stood here an hour earlier; waist deep in the water and now the sand beneath her feet collapses. She runs in place, up the slope of tumbling sand, pumping her boney legs and arms through the water, five seconds that feel like five minutes and she's on the beach wet to her ears. She joins her grandfather by their towels; he's reading a romance novel.

In high school her father had pulled his best friend out of the same river, his arms and legs limp. He dived in head first, the river floor shallow where it used to be deep.

They come here every summer.

Her mother warned her about the currents. The swell had taken her cousin, only about four, twirling a branch in the water, poking it deep under the surface, the sudden hard flow of the water yanking the branch and the girl off the shore. The river rushing her away, her wool coat pulling her deeper as her head bobbed up and down above the waves, her small body fighting to float.

mixed drinks

Basement storage, floor-to-ceiling shelving, rows and rows of glass jars. A bar stacked with alcohol preserved specimens. Jars with fish—black bass and minnows—turtles and birds and mice in ethanol. You sit back in an armchair, reach for a crystal decanter and pour a drink. Gin and tonic and fetus. Cockatiel cocktails. Vodka and canary. Shrewdriver. Take a long sip, chew. Two cubes of ice.

rigor mortis

Her legs, second position. Arms above her head, curved at the elbows, confined to the floor of her apartment. The music starts. Her first time in front of an audience. Blue, sparkly tutu, ballet slippers, she follows the girl in front of her onto the stage. Lights hit her eyes and she scans the audience for her mother, somewhere among the ghosted faces. First position, heels together, plié. The floor of her apartment as cold as her skin, skin stiff, stiff muscles. Her muscles stiff rubber from the hours of practicing her plié. Another girl pulls her hand, pulls towards stage left, wades through the lights, the music heavy against her temples, her knees shake, the room pirouettes. Her heartbeat echoes throughout the hardwood.

wendigo

She picks a spot on the dance floor, swings her arms out, claims the space. Spots him spot her swinging her hips to the bass the strobe light reflects the sweat on her clavicle. Extends her hand each finger points his direction and lingers until the floorboards vibrate up through the arches of his feet shuffle closer. Clammy palms kiss, embrace his neck her waist her hips—firmly her hips—fingertips lift his chin lick. Parched tongue traces chapped lips, opens his mouth, the song changes. She excuses herself to the bar.

origami

At four, she conducted funerals. Started in the front
yard when she found a dead squirrel lying with its
back against the curb. Her father wrapped the body
in a dishcloth and dug a foot-deep hole in the garden.
She stood over the mound of dirt, waved her hands
in sharp staccato like she'd seen at the orchestra,
placed a dandelion on the grave, bowed her head.

All summer she sat on the edge of her driveway,
giving funerals to ants and beetles and earwigs,
worms she found dead on the sidewalk and flies from
her windowsill. She buried them under a brick she
decorated with fresh yellow dandelions, her secret
cemetery. At eight, she learned to fold boxes out of
construction paper, made them in different colours
and sizes. Boxes with lids and boxes without lids, a
small dab of glue to hold the sides together. Lined
up her creations on a table by the sidewalk, asked
her mother to write a sign for "bug coffins." Her
mother wrote "origami boxes" and she sold them to
her neighbours for twenty-five cents.

When she was 15 her beta fish died so she folded a paper container to fit his figure, buried him on top of the squirrel.

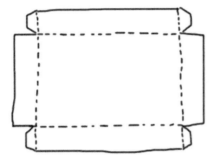

part IV

carbon copy

carbon copy

Two weeks ago a man come into my shop and commissioned a ring made with "the biggest blood diamond I can buy"—his words. I thought he was kidding, but he explained how his wife's skin flushed and shivered from knowing her jewellery carried the price of bodies. He pulled out a cheque book and I told him to get out. I'd faster turn him into a diamond for his wife to wear.

When you got sick one of the neighbours came over with some brochures. She knew I was a jeweller and along with her grief counselling pamphlets she had one advertising a service that turned your loved one's cremated ashes into a diamond. A "memorial to their unique life." Your mother and I told her it wasn't necessary, and fatal wasn't in our vocabulary, but she left the leaflets in a neat pile on the kitchen table, rubbed her palm against my shoulder and said, "I know it must be hard, but it's better to prepare."

You're in the hospital two cities away and they're killing your cancer (and your carbon coloured hair) with heavy radiation. I've been matched as a donor, great news, but the transplant means the doctor's desperate. Still, when you play with the other children the nurses overhear you whisper, "my daddy is my medicine." I told you I would fill your bones with titanium if it were possible; titanium the strongest metal. You told me you liked silver better because it came from the stars.

And there are days when I think why not, why not cook you into a flawless diamond your mother can wear around her finger? It's not any more ludicrous than sitting you on a mantle in a ceramic jar your mother made at pottery class or burying you underground where we'll visit a rectangular piece of earth four times a year. Instead of a wooden coffin I'll buy a velvet ring box. *A memorial to your unique life*, indistinguishable from the billions of diamonds stock-piled in De Beers warehouses, only a handful released each year. Dear Cecil, when you began buying up all the small diamond mines in Africa did you ever stop and think about daughters? An exclusive conference room and men with suits and magnifying glasses buying diamond-packaged daughters. And Cecil, what about those advertising campaigns? Deceiving daughters into believing that love could be mined from the earth, and without carats there can be no "I dos" because a diamond is and a diamond is. And Cecil? How did you feel when you learned a chemist could recreate a diamond from scratch? It's debatable whether an experienced jeweller can tell apart a real versus synthetic diamond, and most people can't tell apart zirconia. Laboratory built jewels with faultlessly polished faces. Carbon, pressure, semen: can you cook a daughter the same way you cook a diamond? A diamond with no blemishes the ultimate symbol of perfection. Object daughter. If I make you into a diamond will the cancer be a microscopic fleck etched underneath your surface? A woman at the doctor's office told me, "you're still young, you'll have better luck with the next one." My fist a rock I wanted to plunge into the magazine rack. I always drive the long way, avoid the cemetery.

After your diagnoses I couldn't make watches anymore. Crafting a gold band with a large hole in it felt cruel, just a big empty space where time was supposed to be. Yours the first I've made in 17 months. Silver, of course, with little white crystals all around the band. Among the crystals I hid one diamond.

I don't even know if you'll ever learn how to tell the time.

> hold you on my knee, twist wrap arms around you, press against chest,   lock you up warehouse limited release, you in&exhale, squirm and squirm, I loosen, you slip away, jeté the hospital room floor

acknowledgements

An enormous thank you to:

My friends and family for supporting me, sharing their stories, and letting me distort them into poetry.

My parents for their love, encouragement, and unwavering belief in everything I do.

My sister, who grew up to be my best friend. I feel so lucky.

Michael, the best person I know. You make every day exciting.

Nicole—without you this book would not exist.

My editor, Doug, for his kindness, patience, and enthusiasm.

The entire team at NeWest Press for their hard work and dedication to this project. Matt, Claire, and Kate—thank you.

EMILIA DANIELEWSKA was born in Poland and grew up in Windsor, ON. She holds a Masters in English, Language, Literature, and Creative Writing from the University of Windsor. She currently lives and works in London, England. Her debut poetry book, *Paper Caskets*, is part of the Crow Said Poetry series.